Whore Story

Adorable Swear Word To Color

FOR STRESS RELEASING

By

Cathy Chadson

Happy Coloring

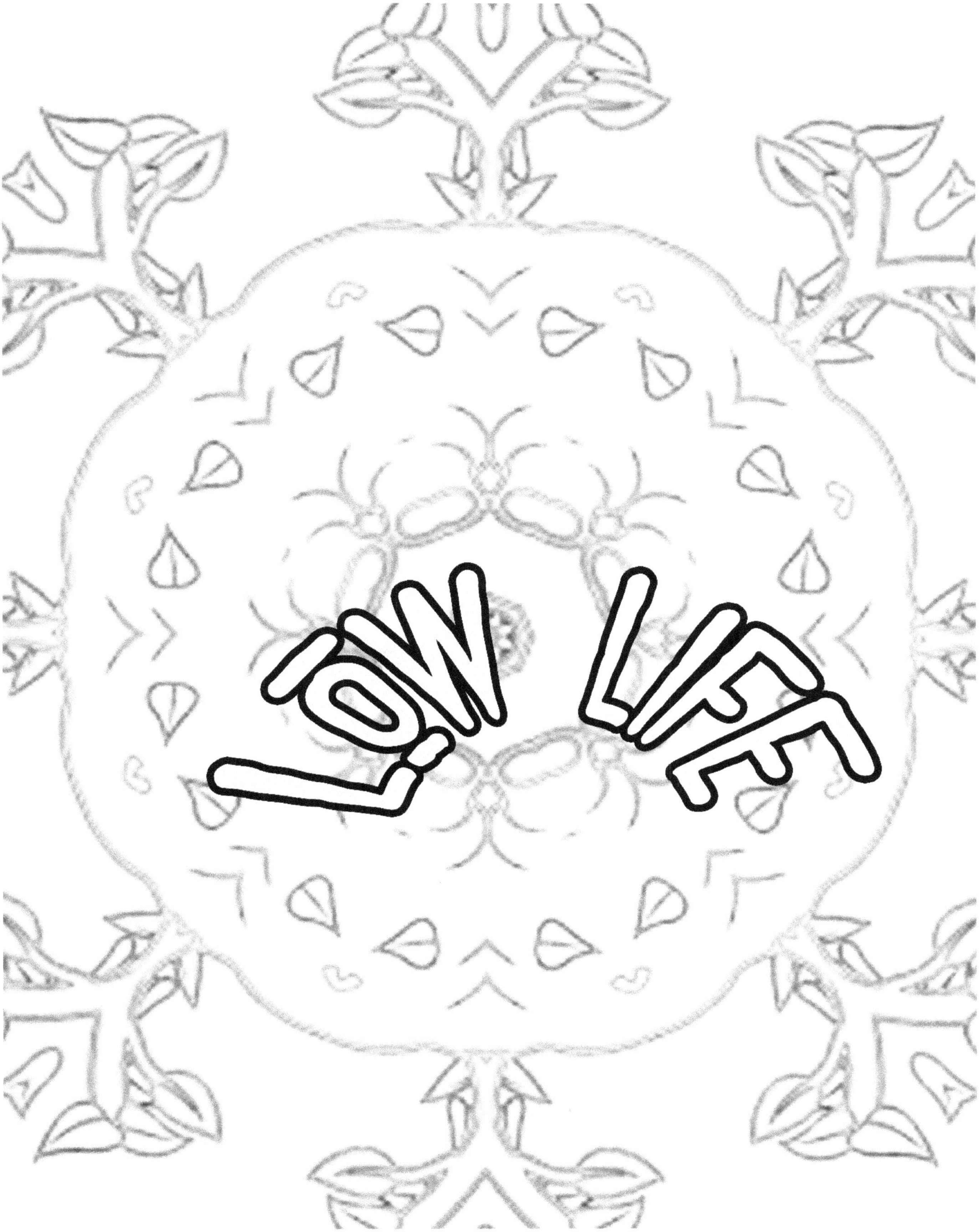
LOW LIFE

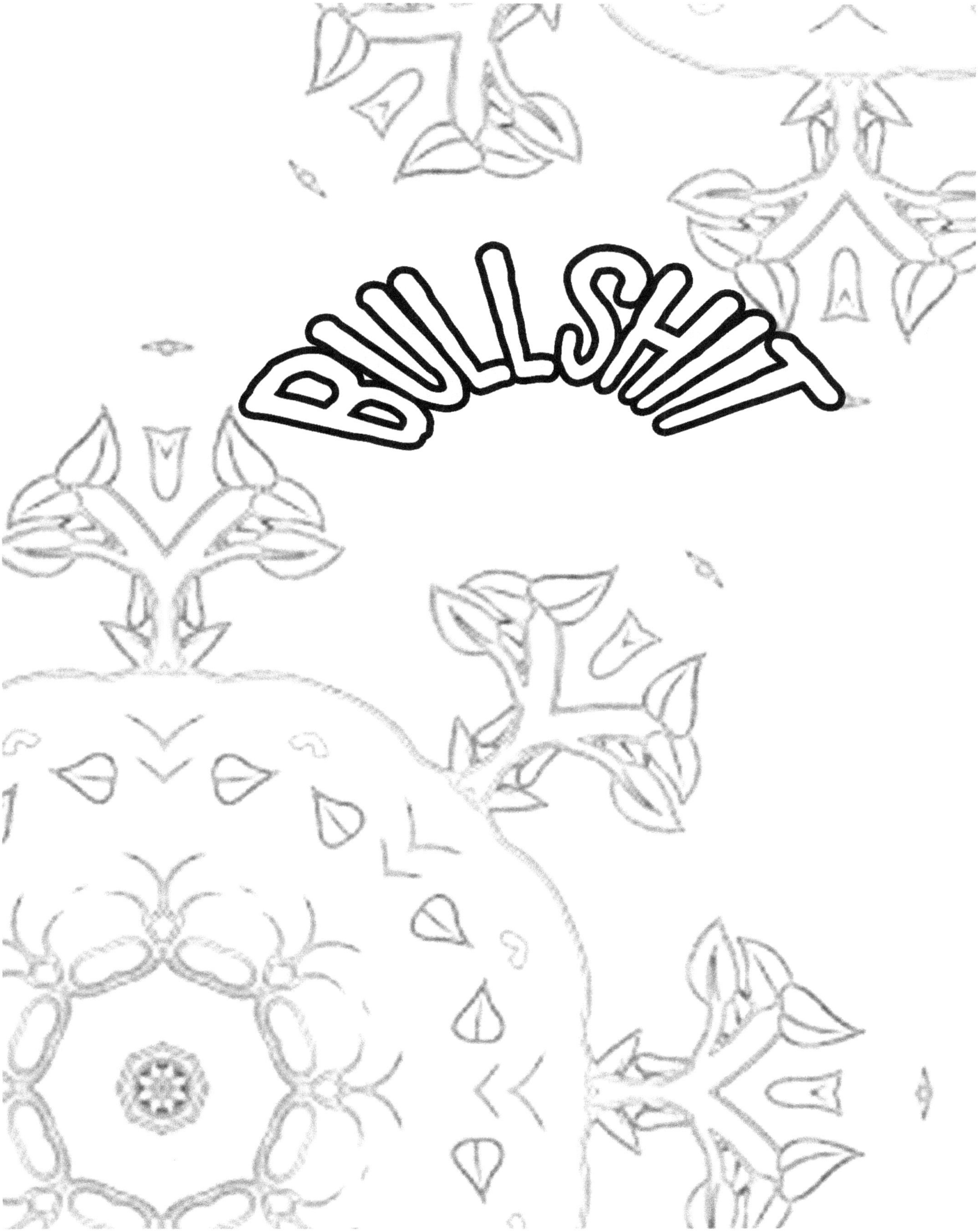
BULLSHIT

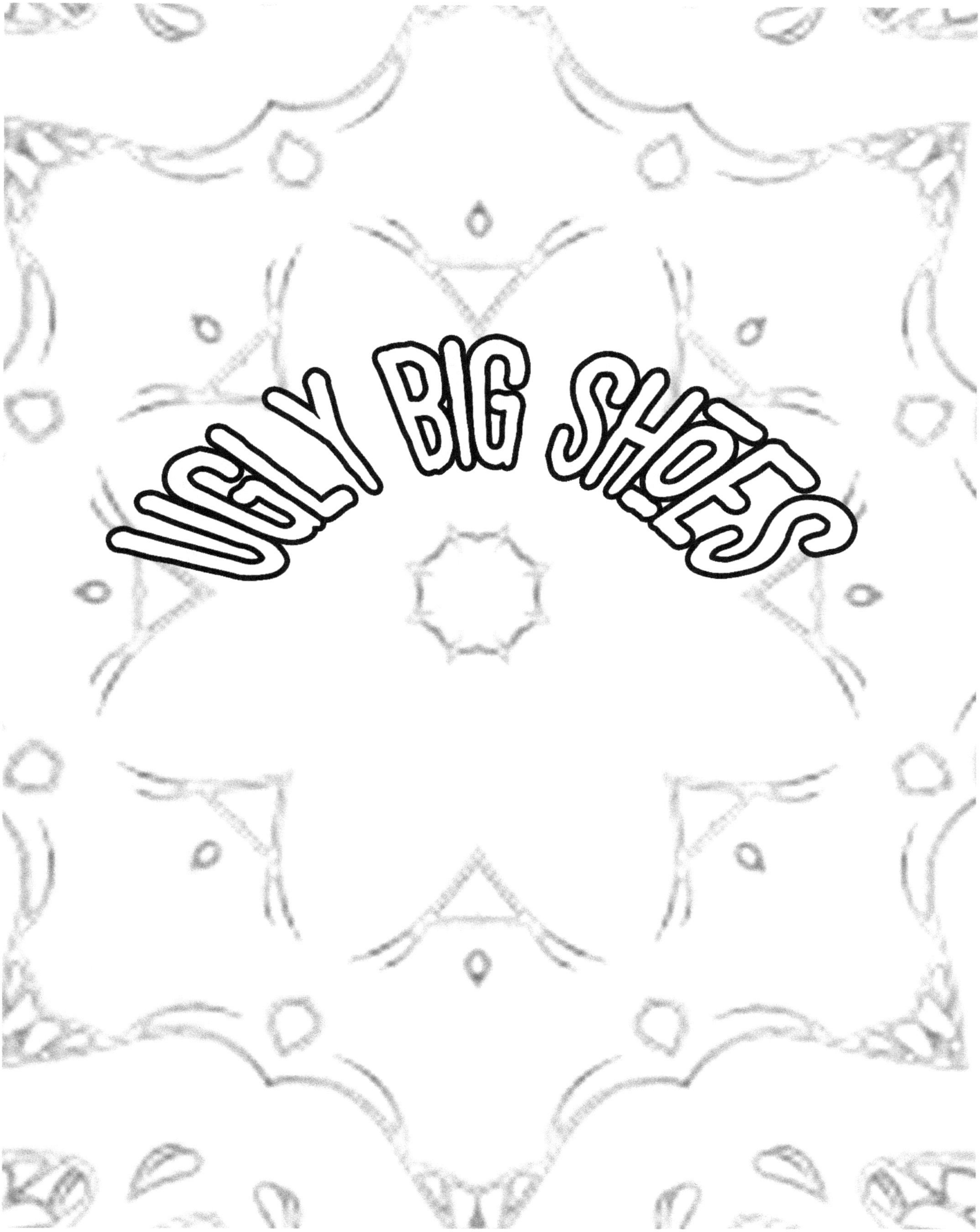
UGLY BIG SHOES

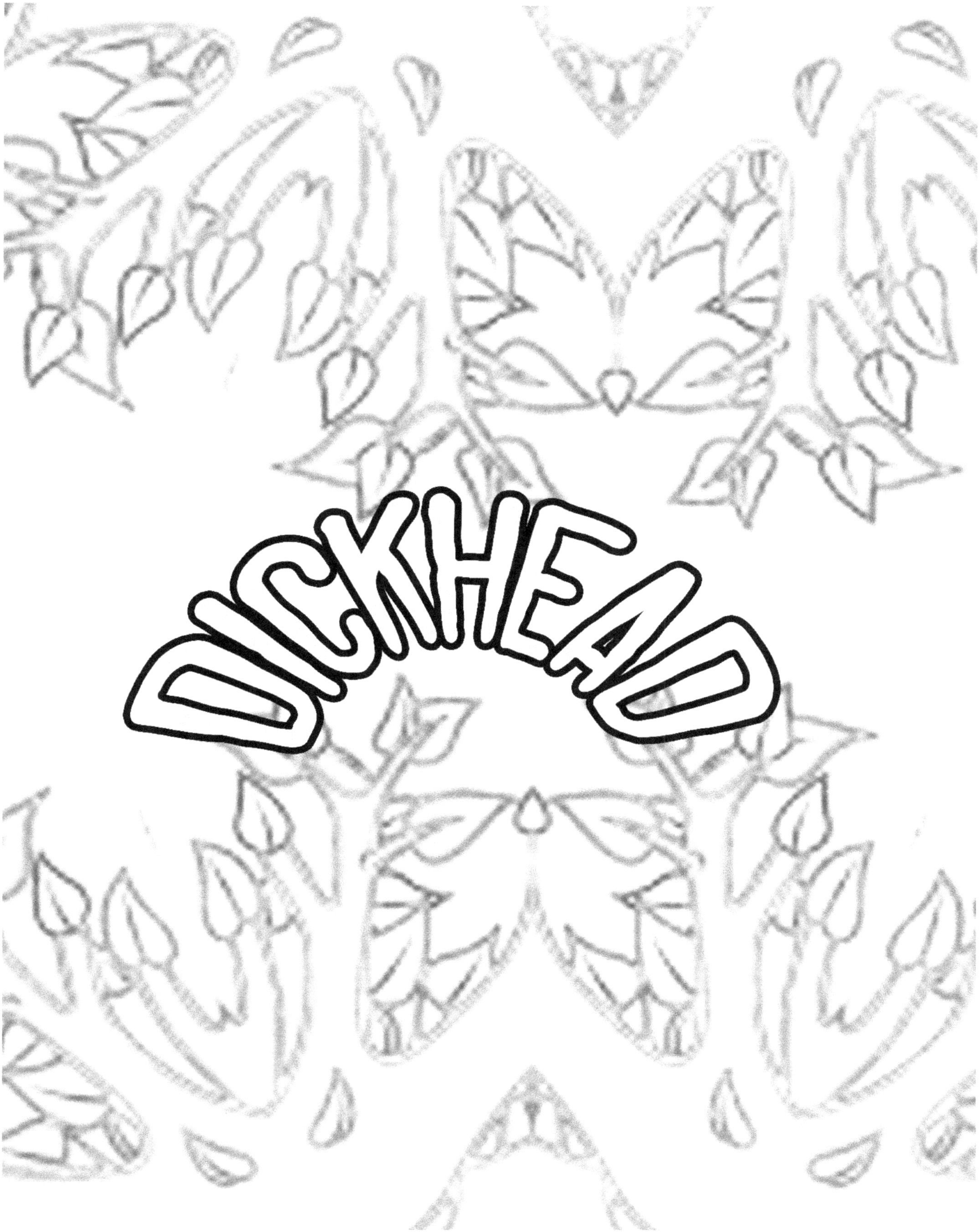
DICKHEAD

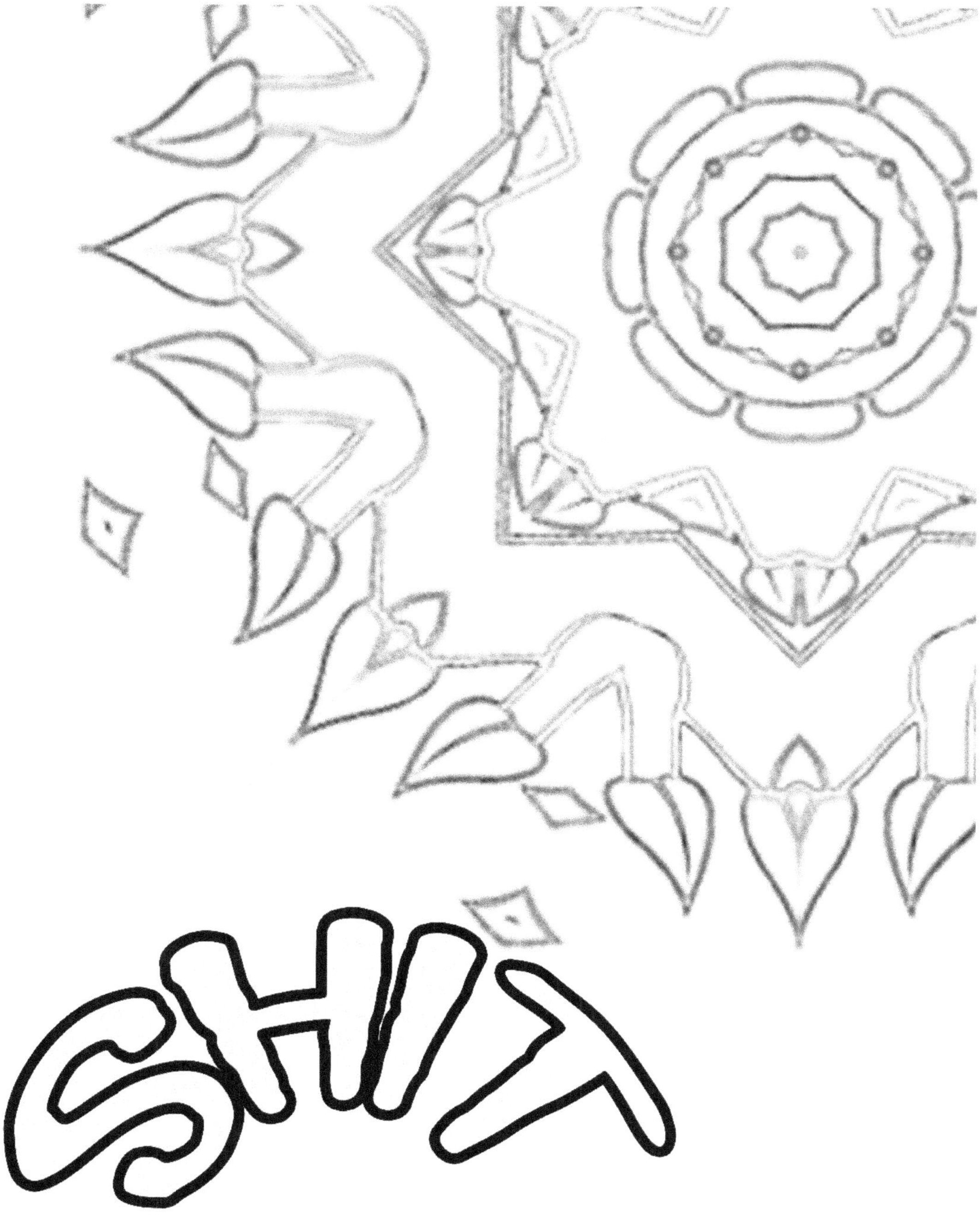
SHIT

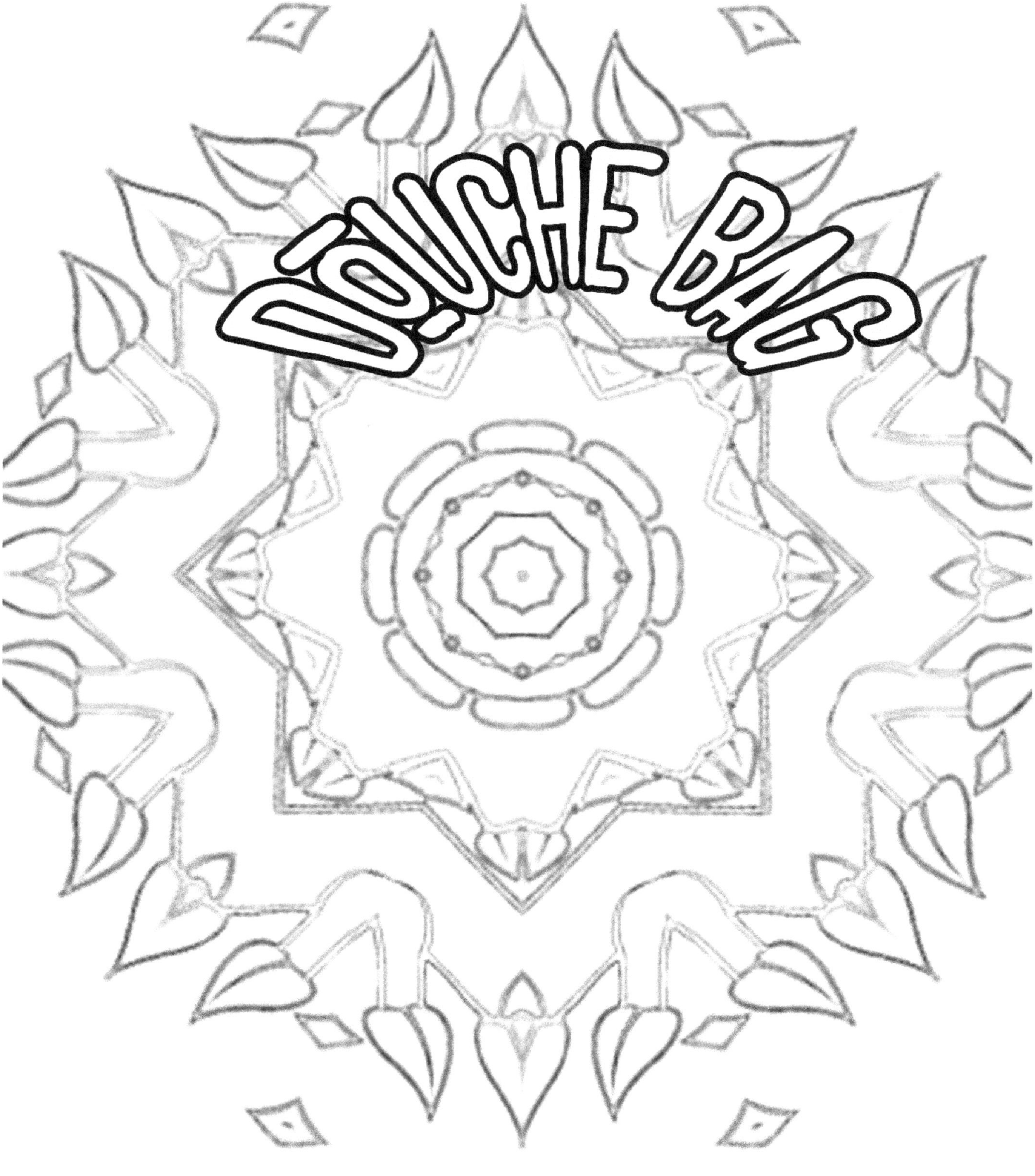
DOUCHE BAG

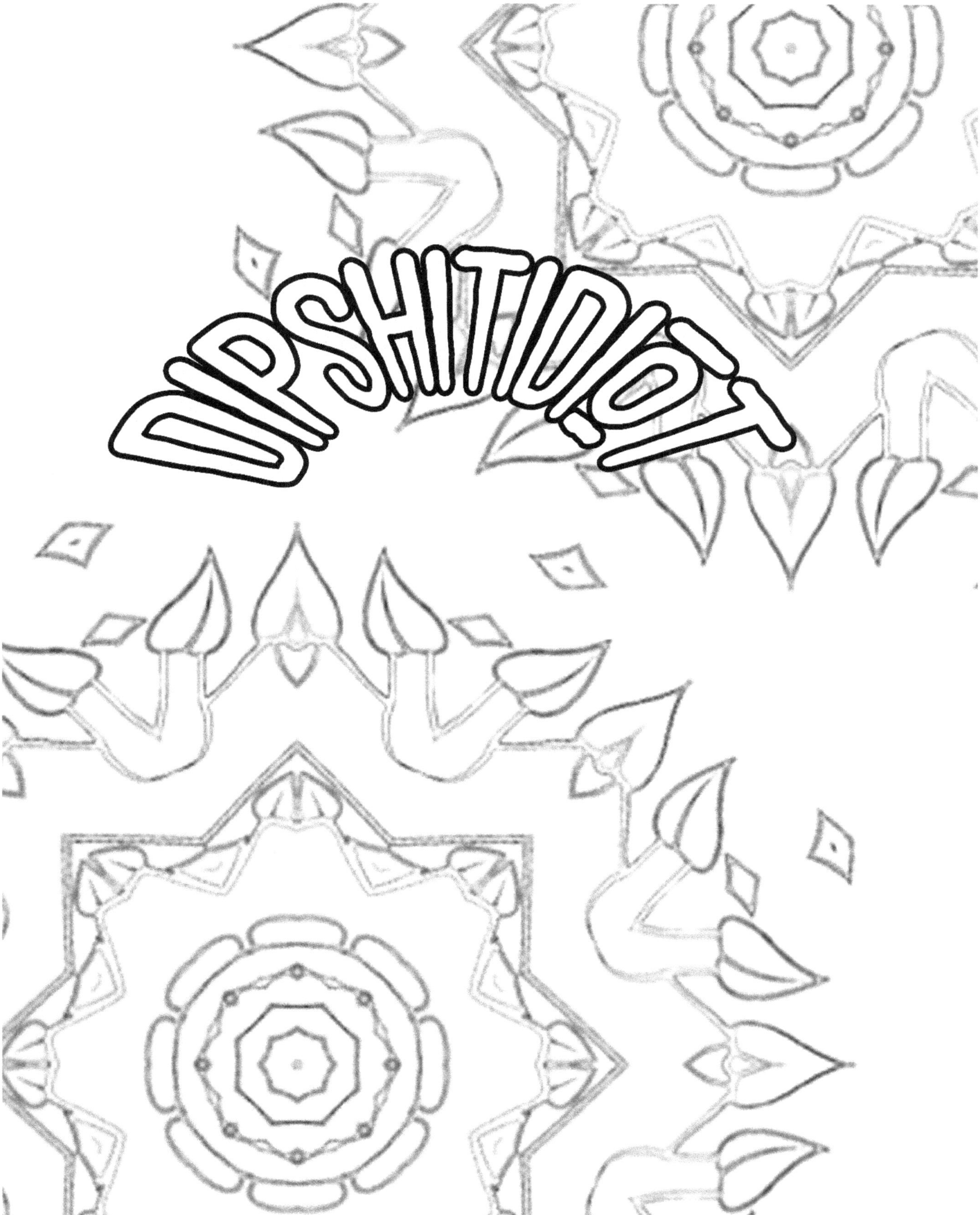
DIPSHITIDIOT

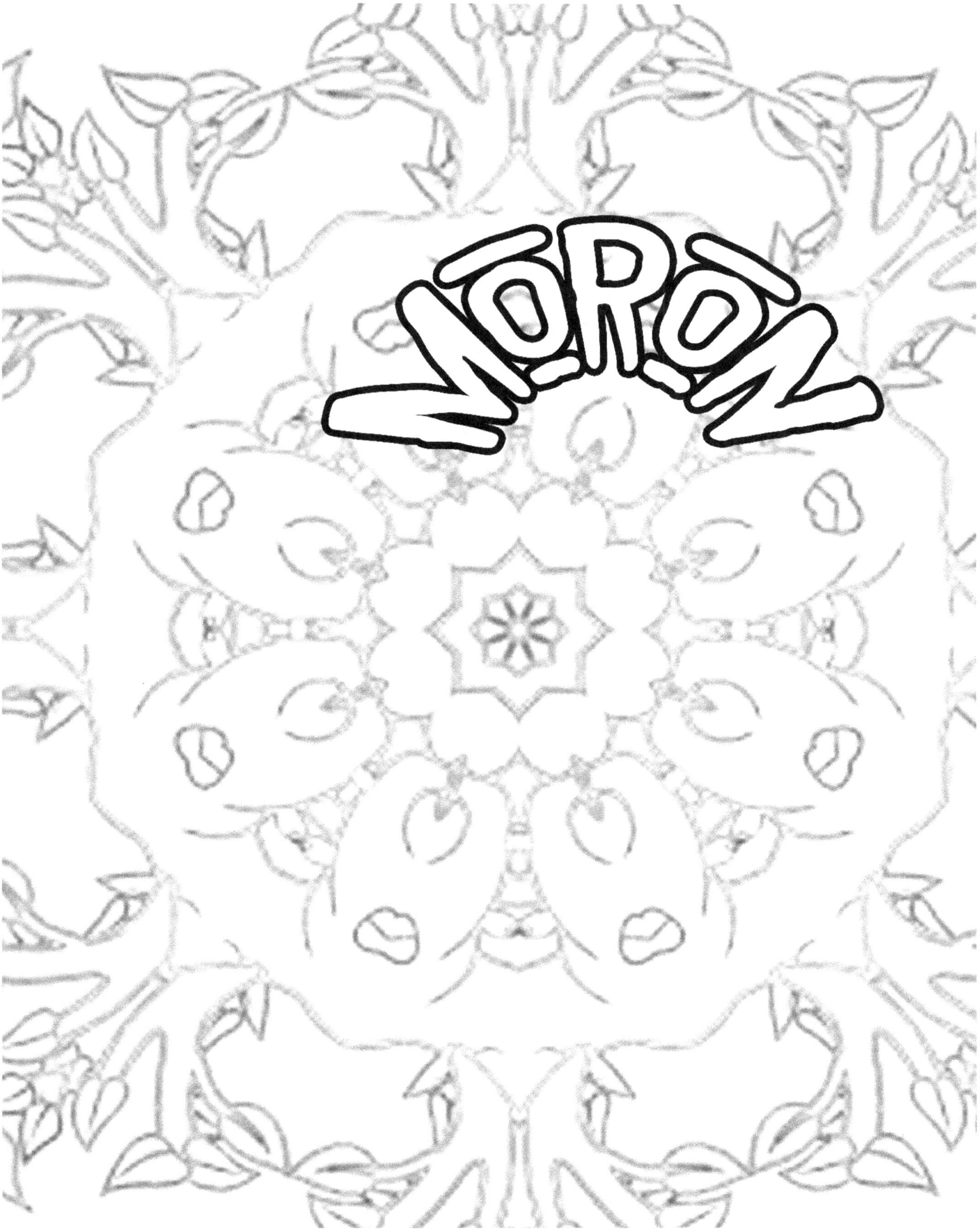
MORON

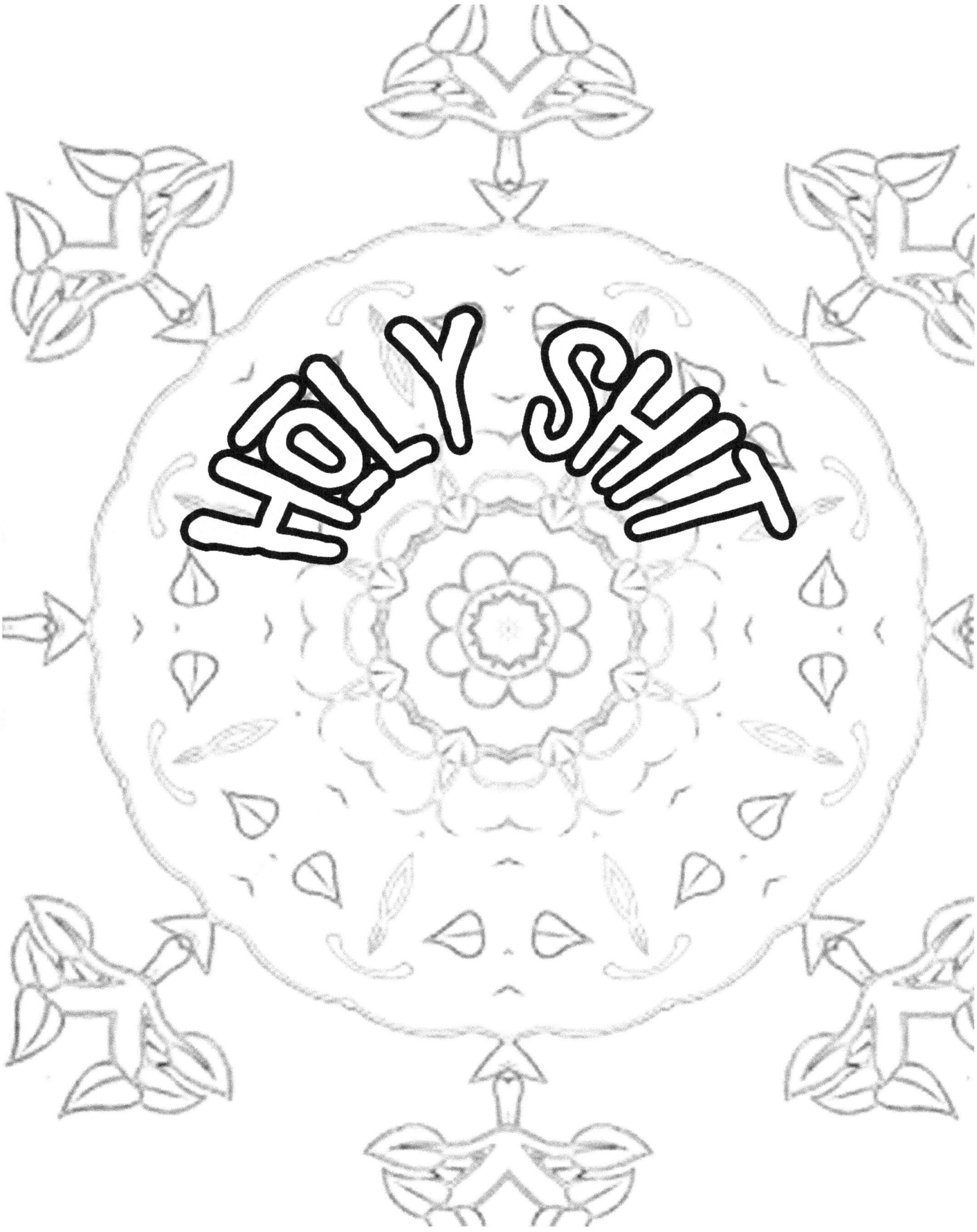
HOLY SHIT

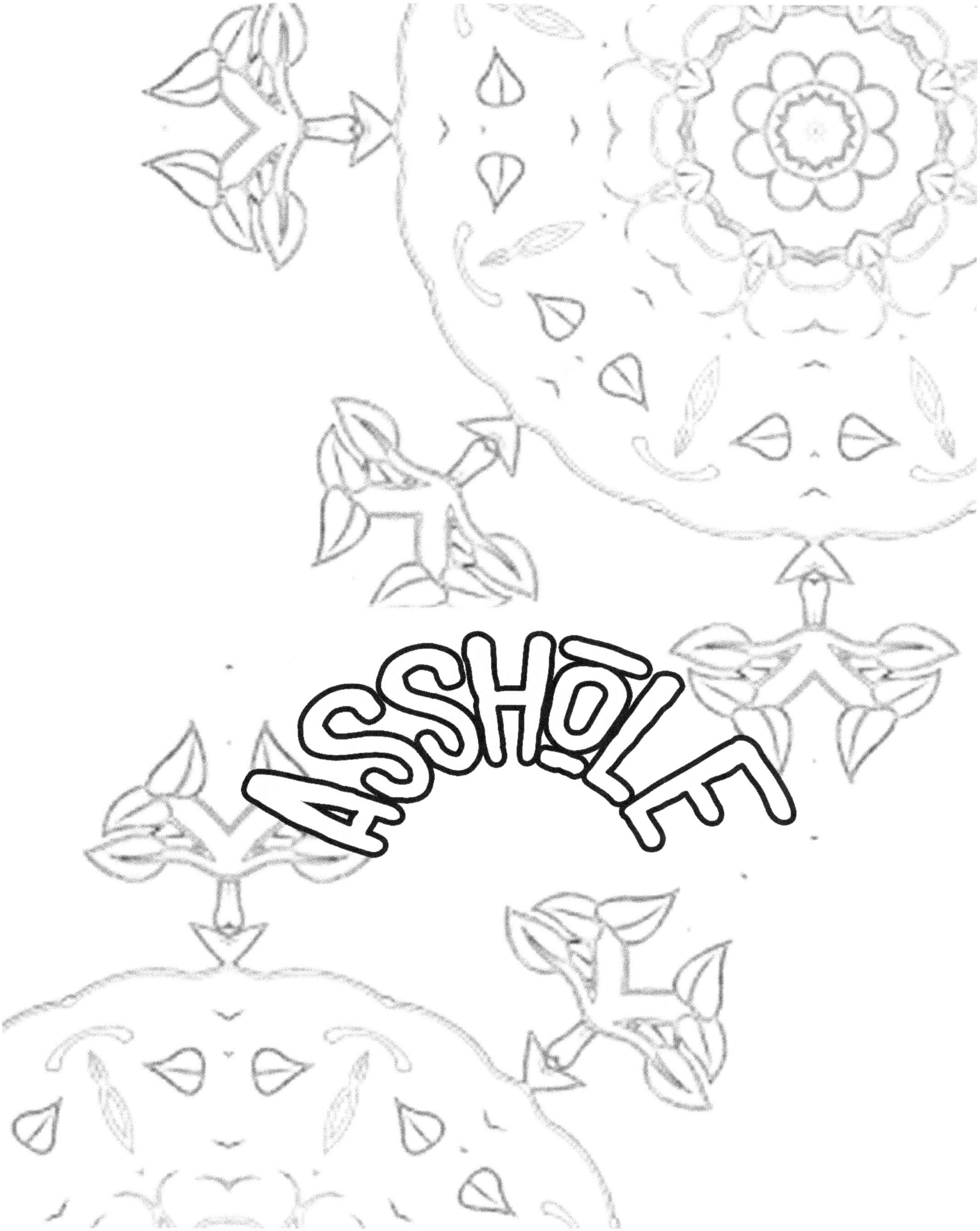
ASSHOLE

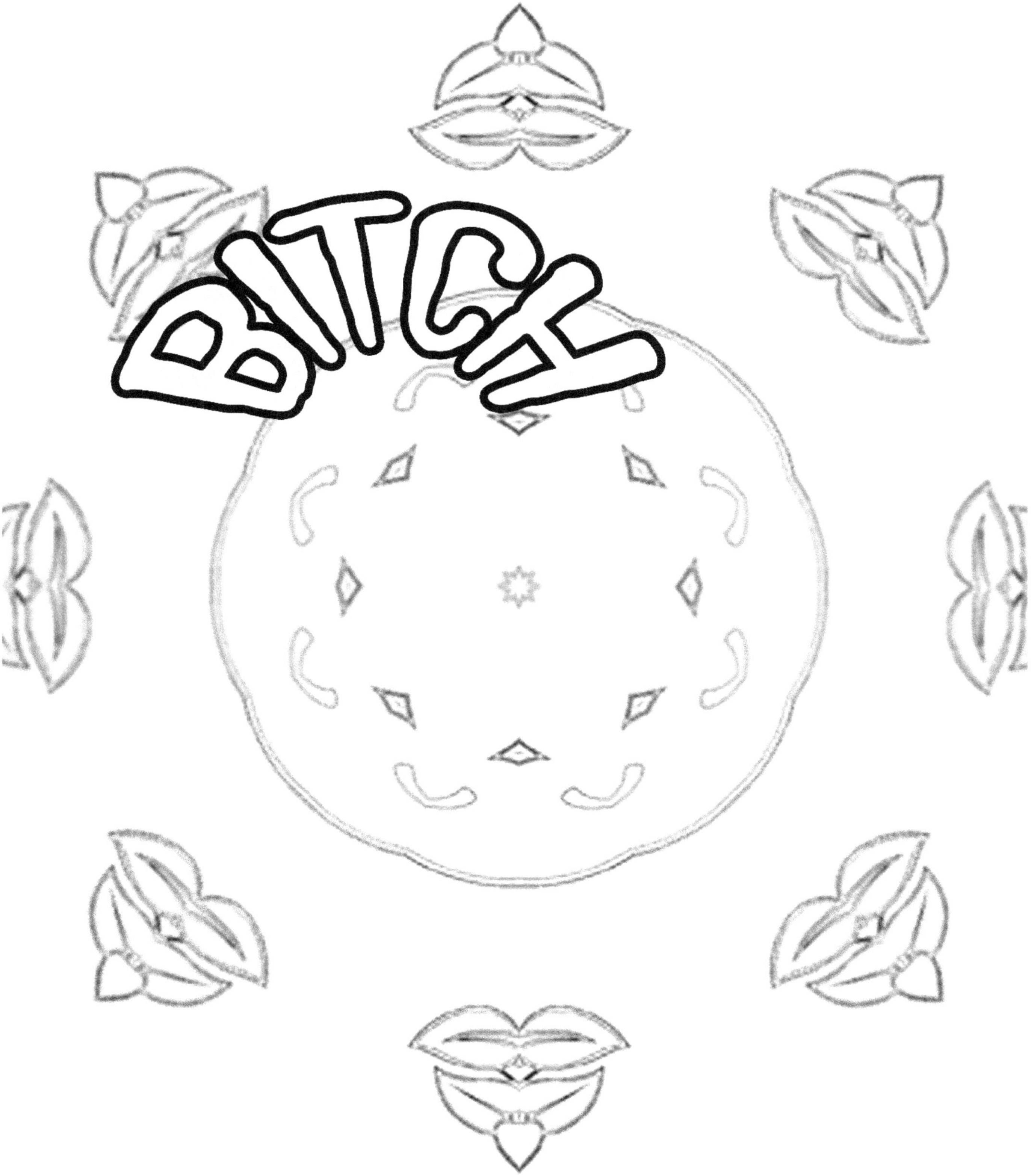
BITCH

BATSHIT CRAZY

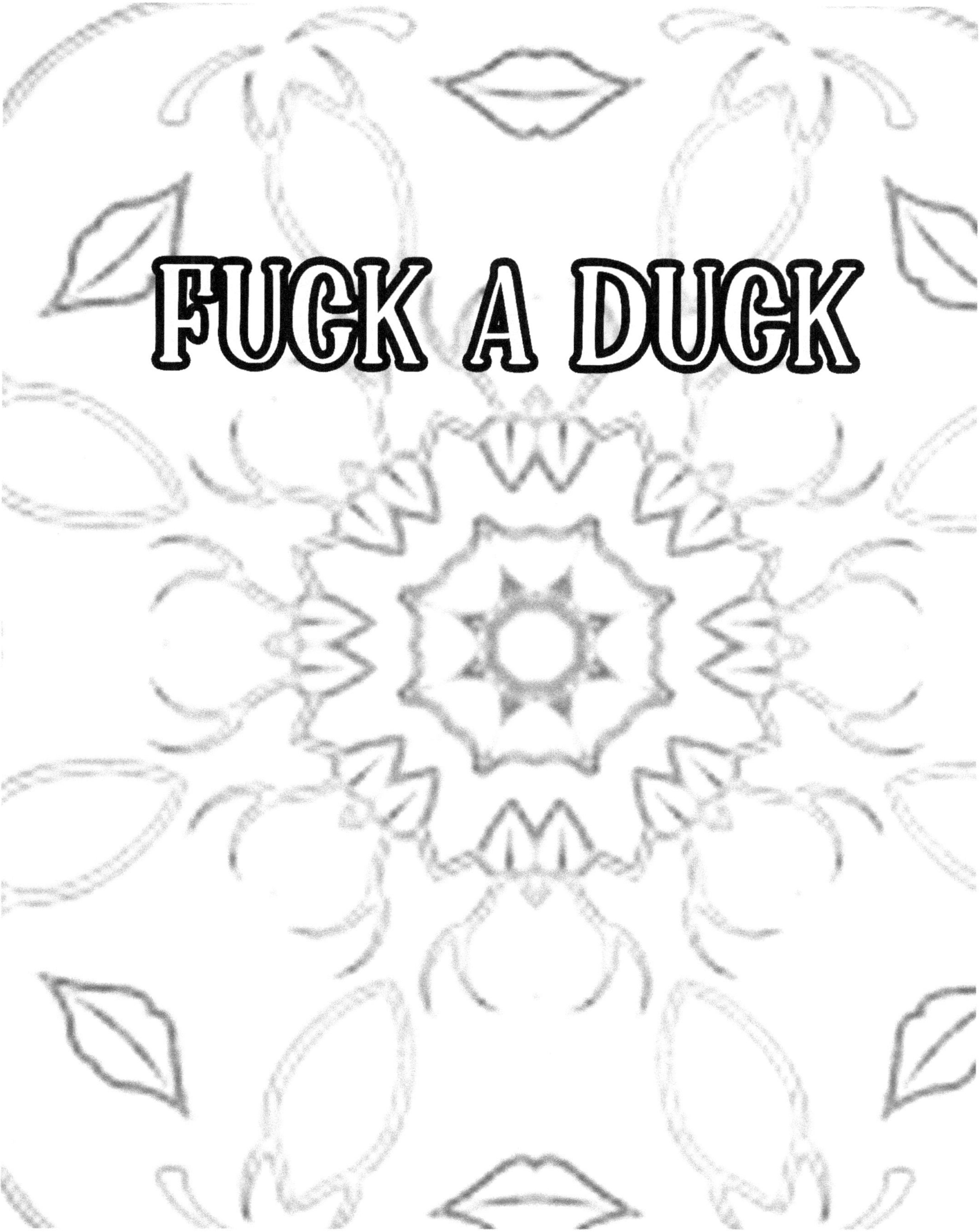
FUCK A DUCK

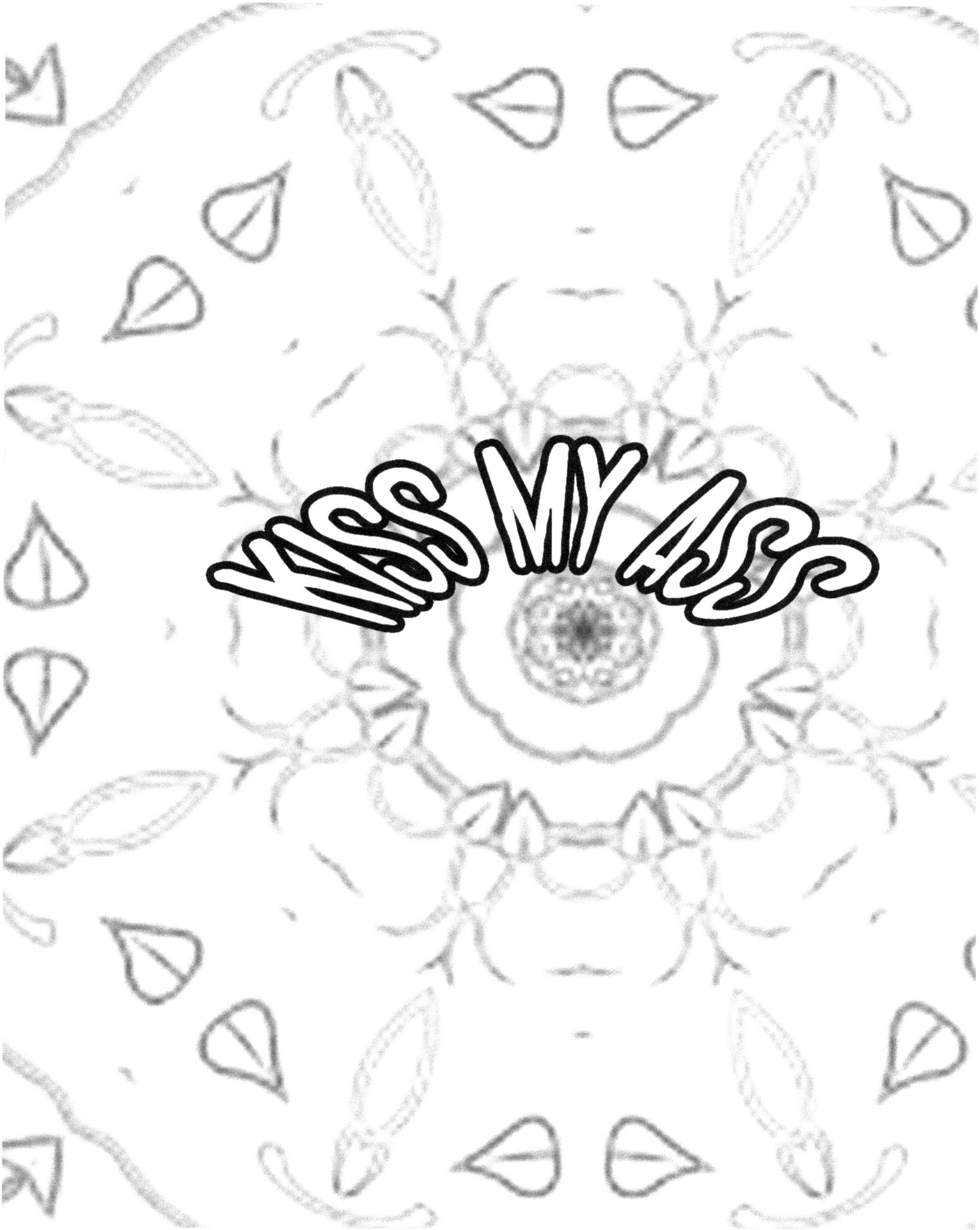
KISS MY ASS

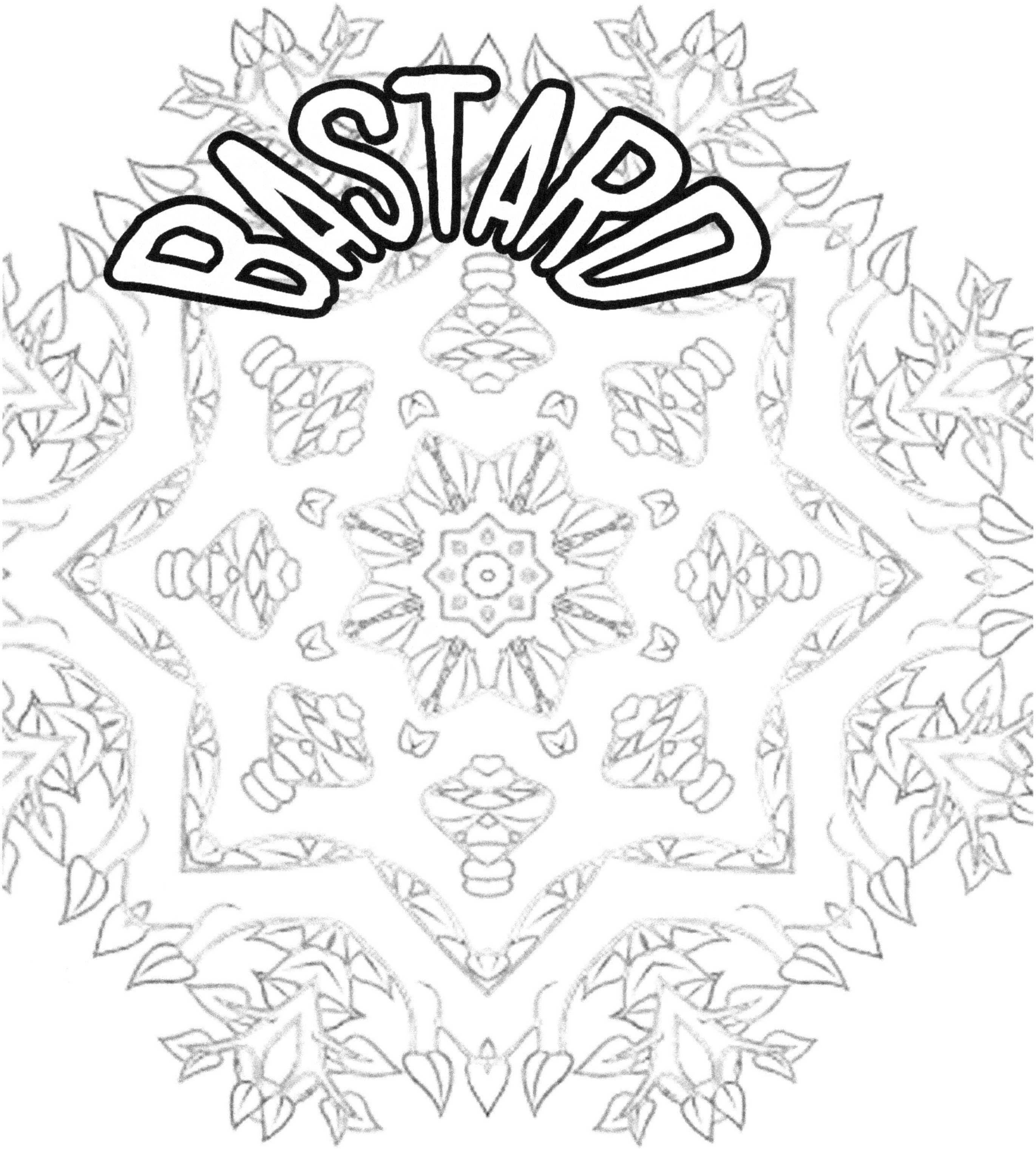
BASTARD

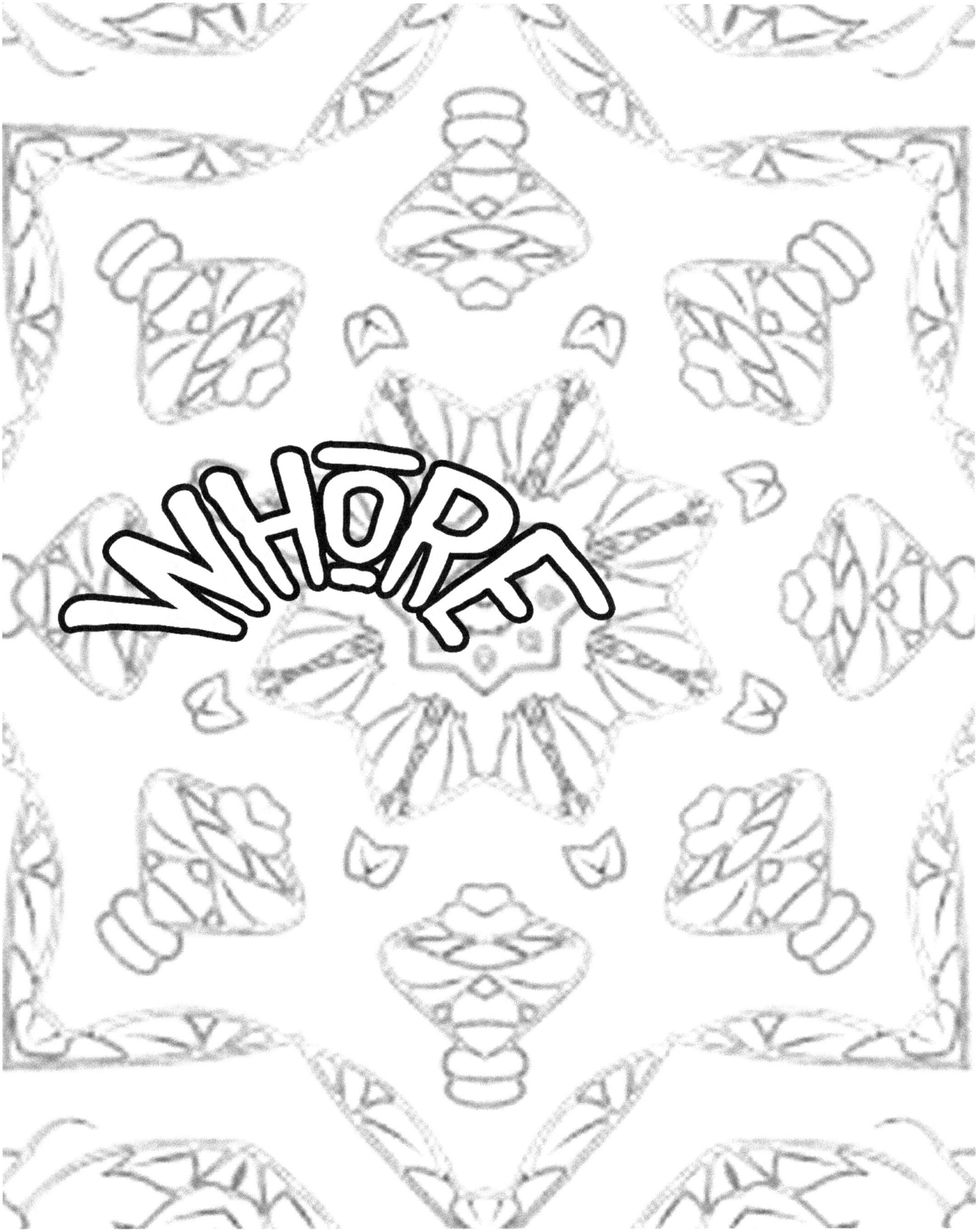
WHORE

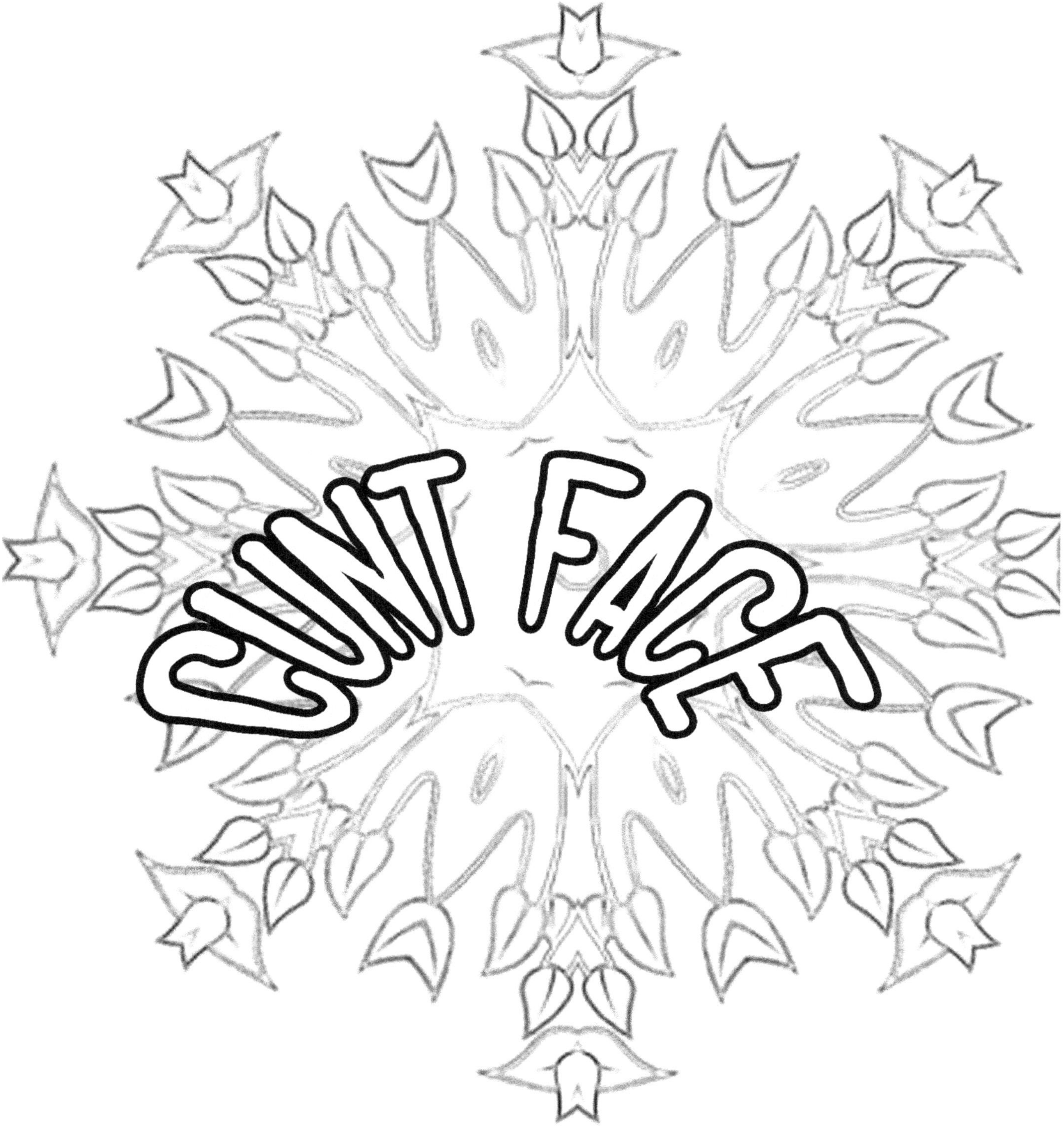
CUNT FACE

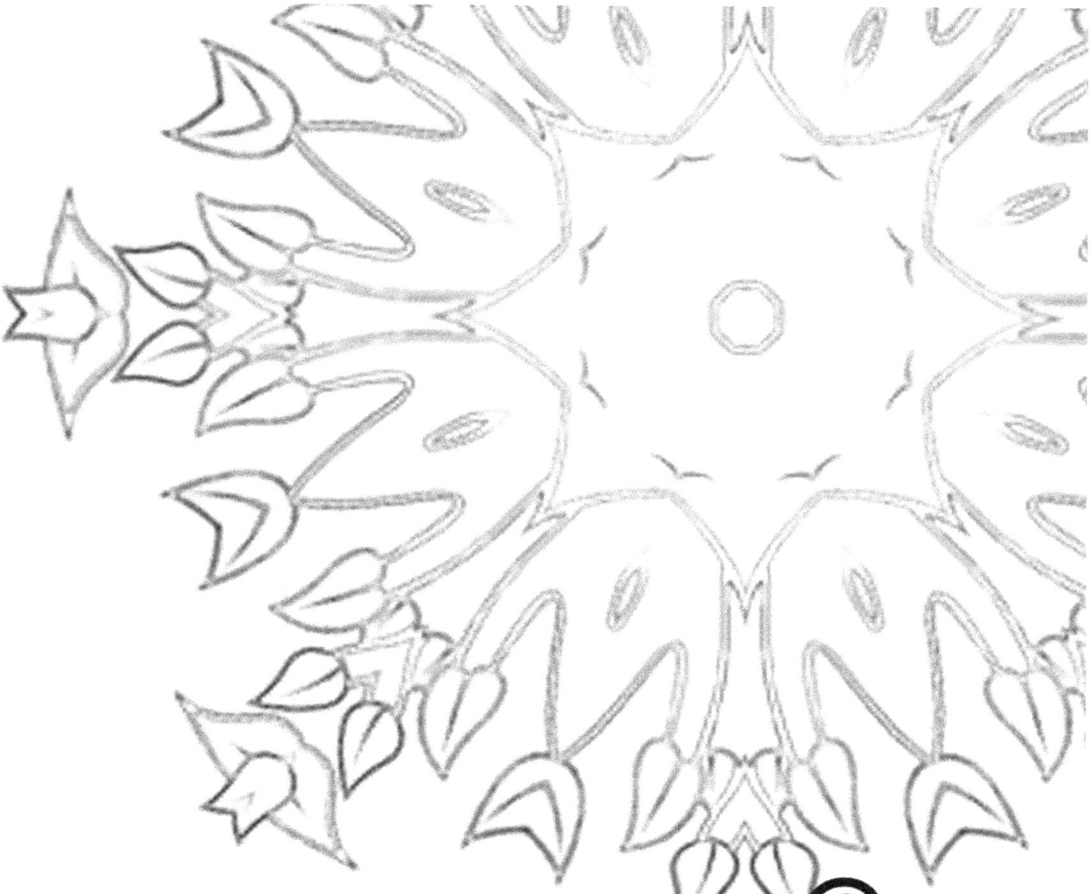

ATTENTION WHORE

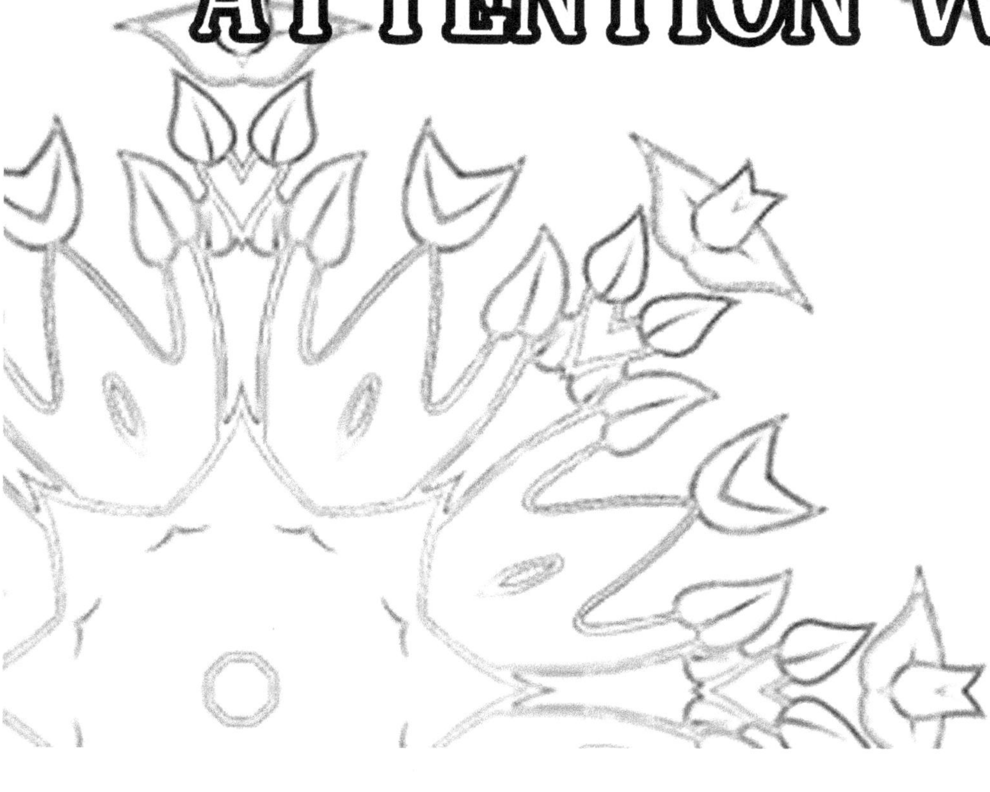

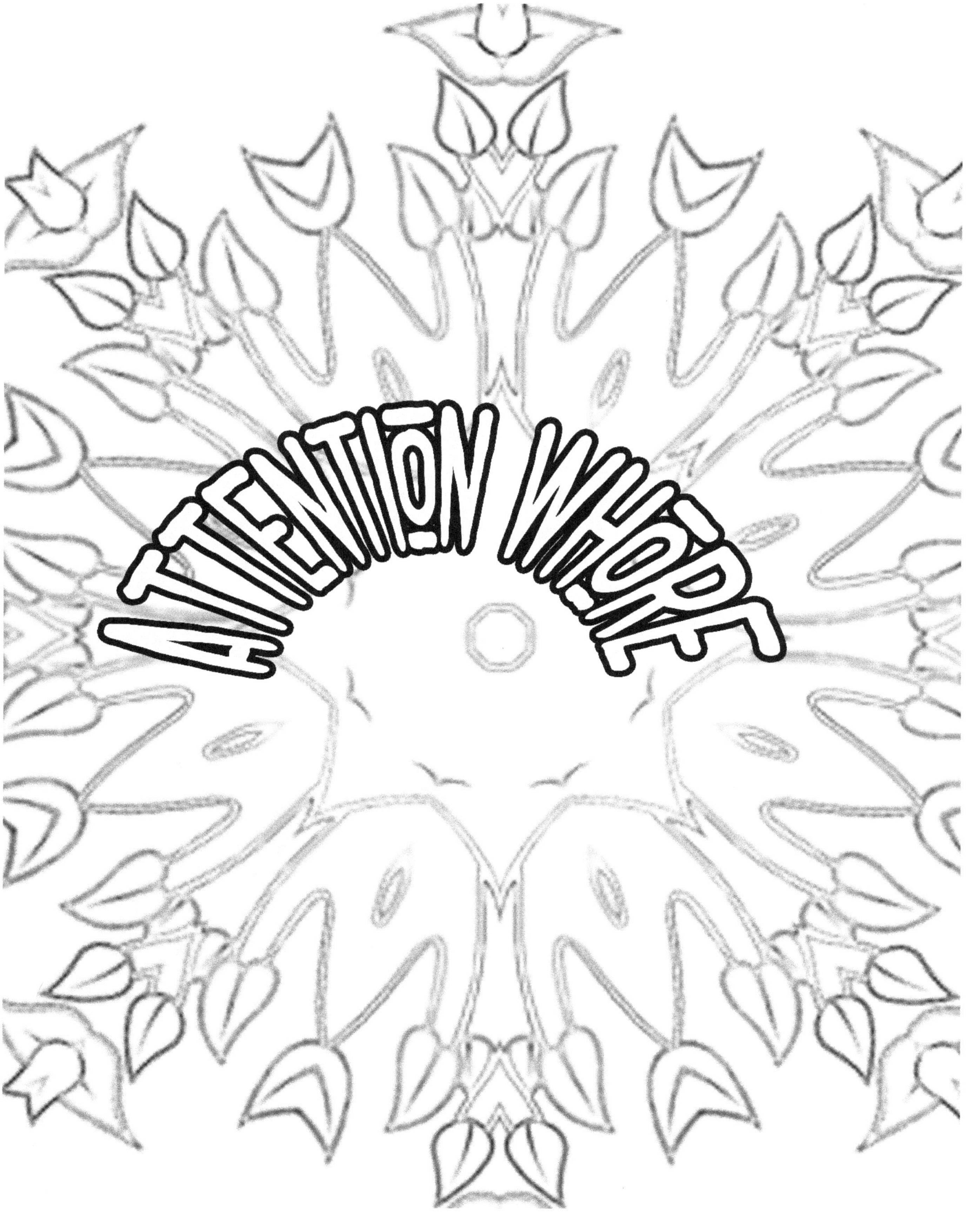
ATTENTION WHORE

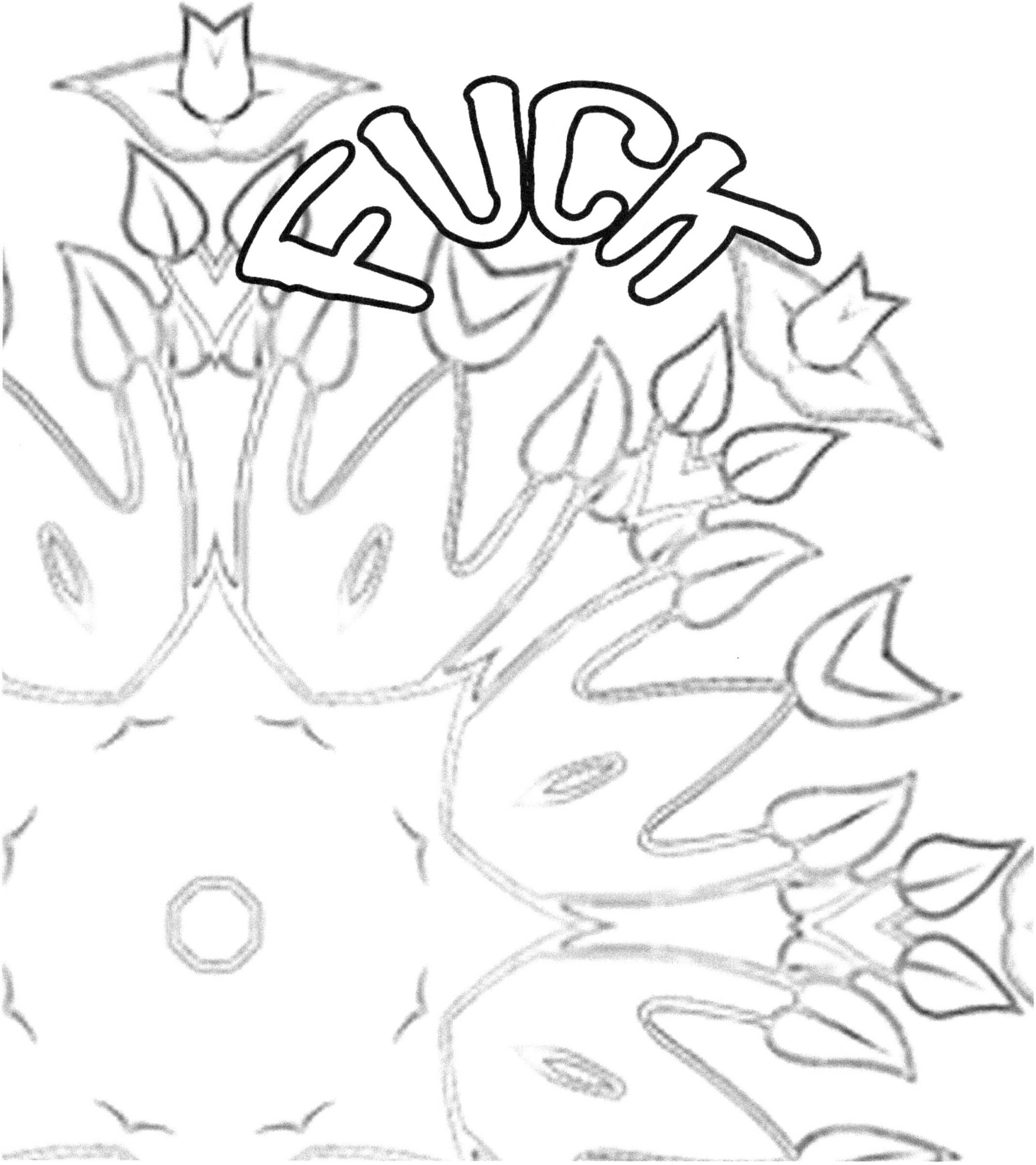
FUCK

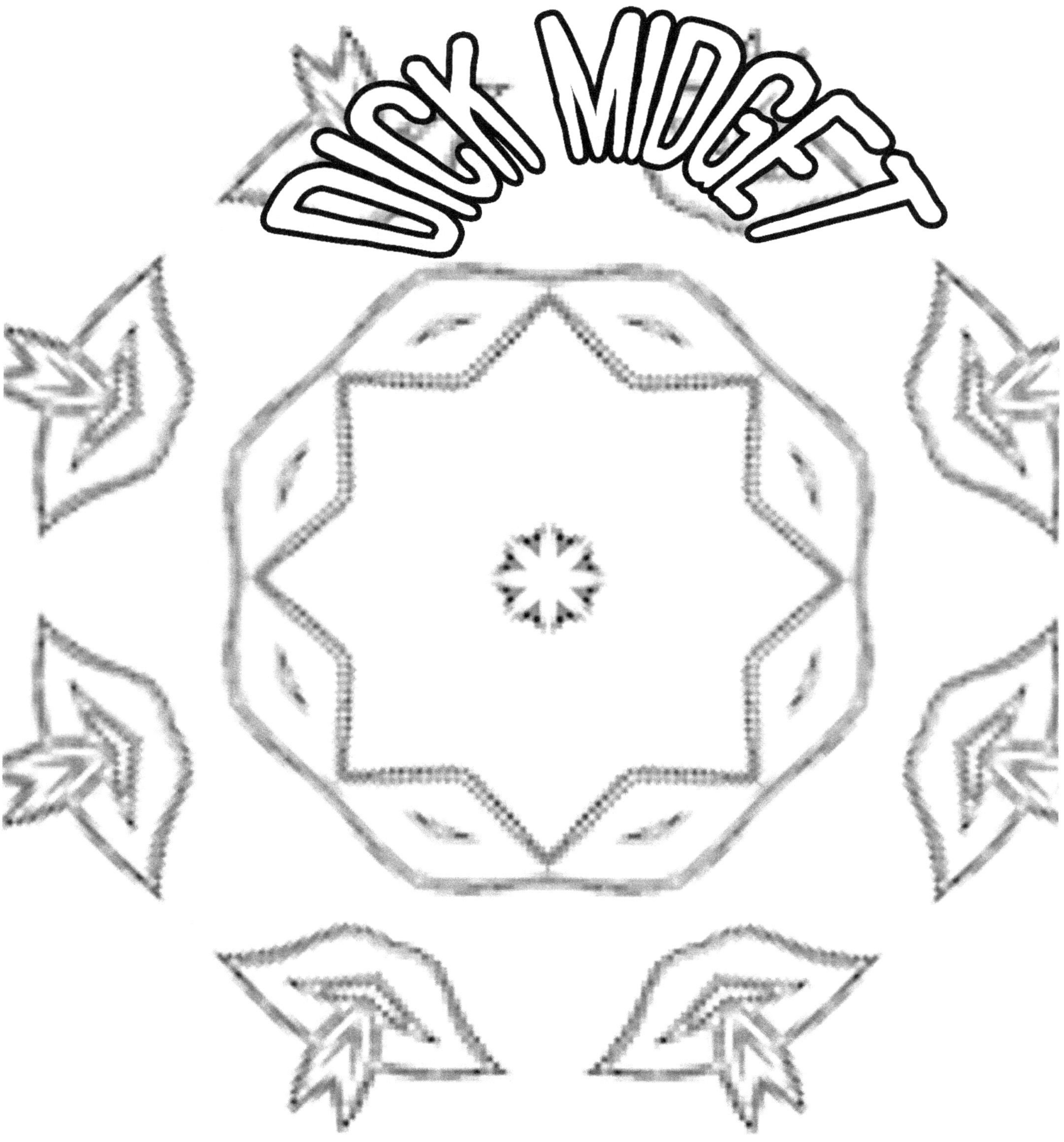
DICK MIDGET

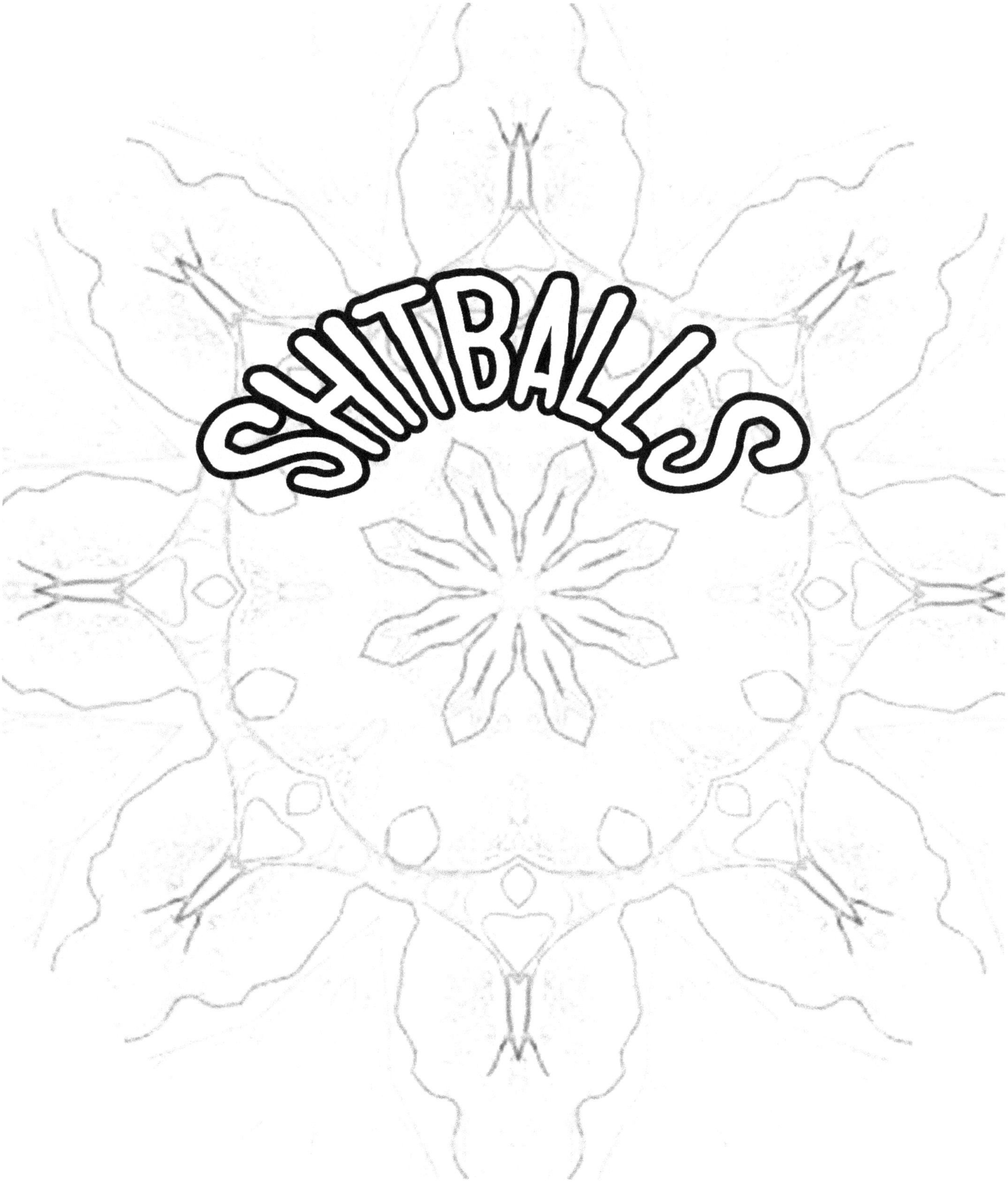
SHITBALLS

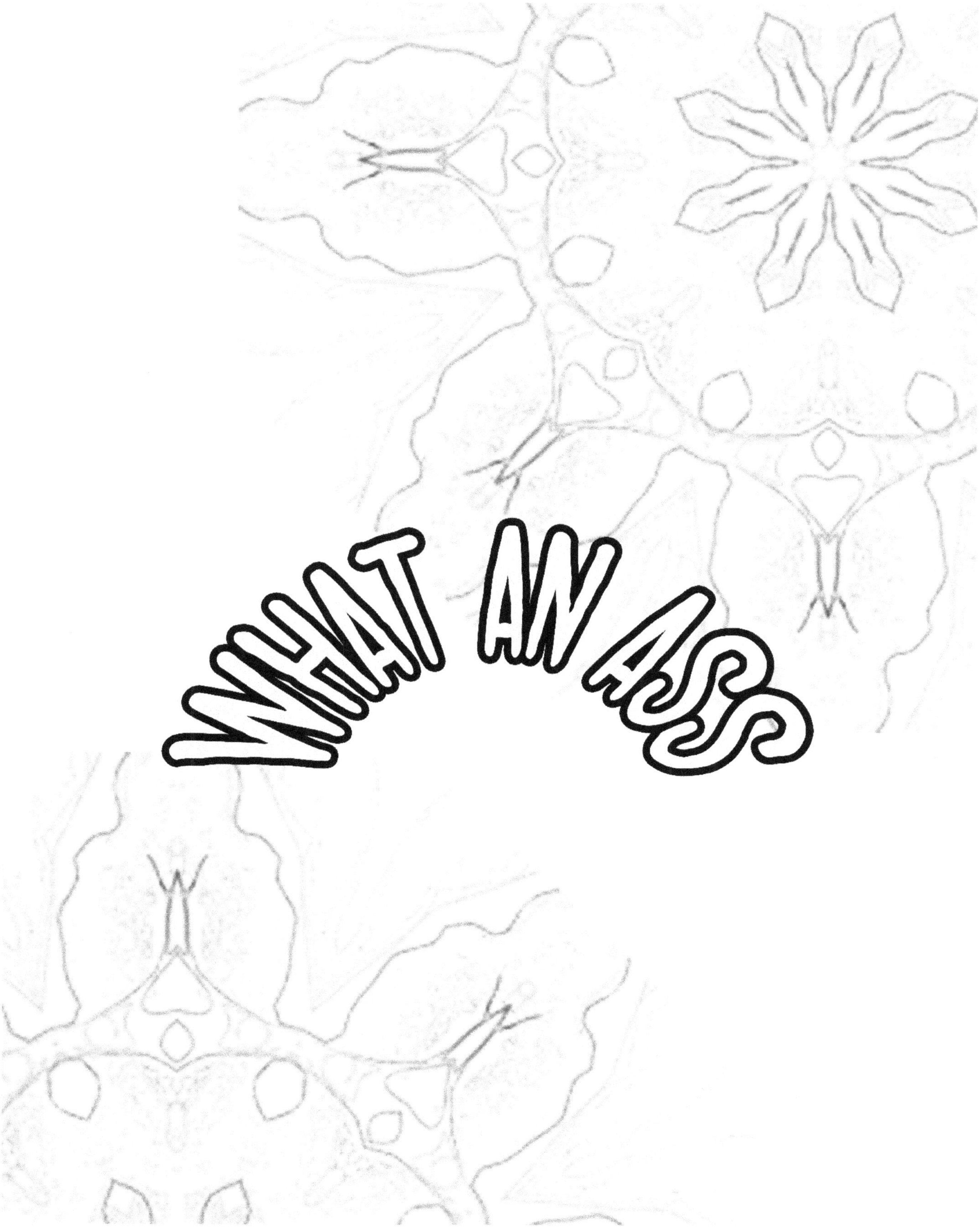
WHAT AN ASS

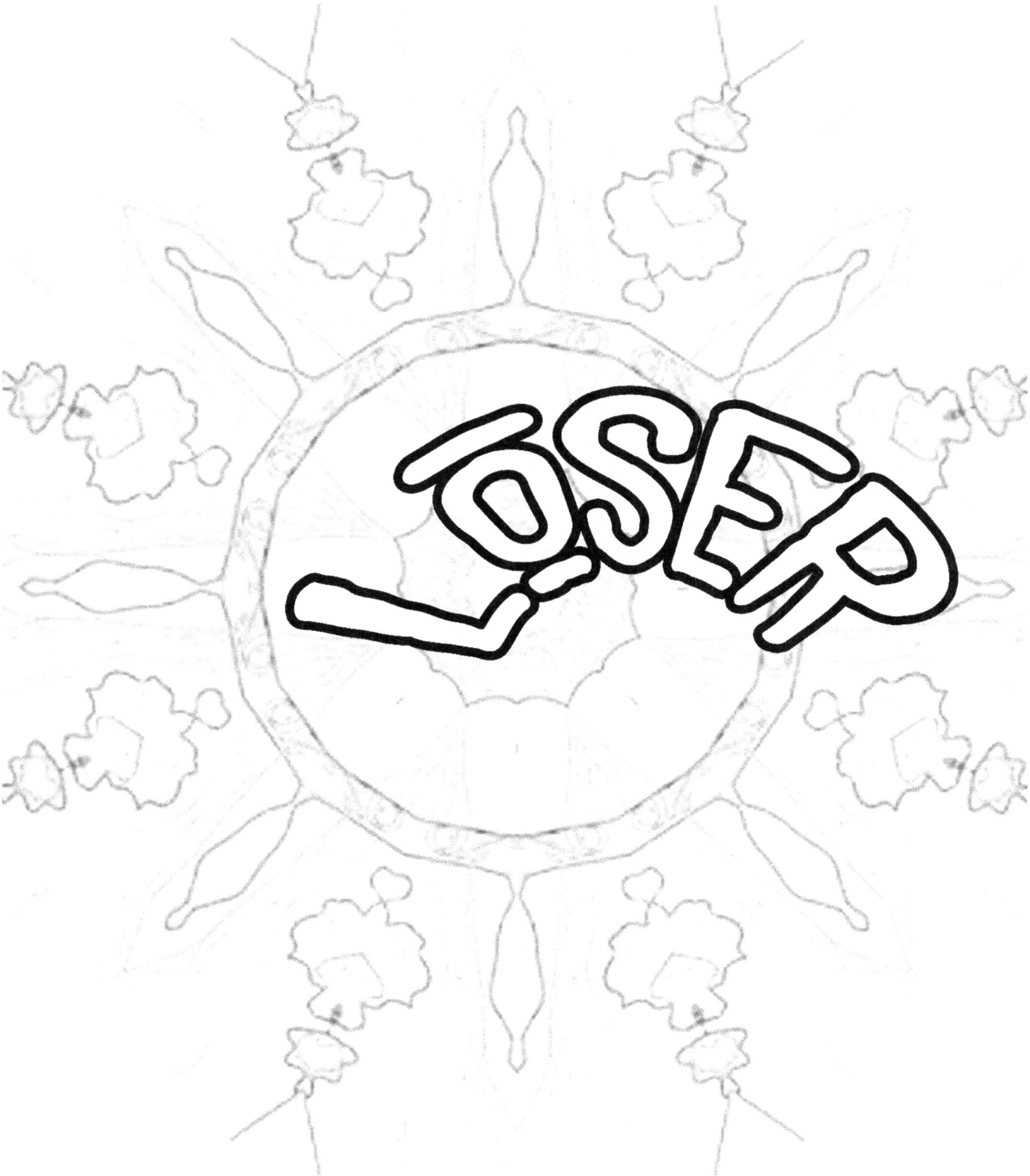
LOSER

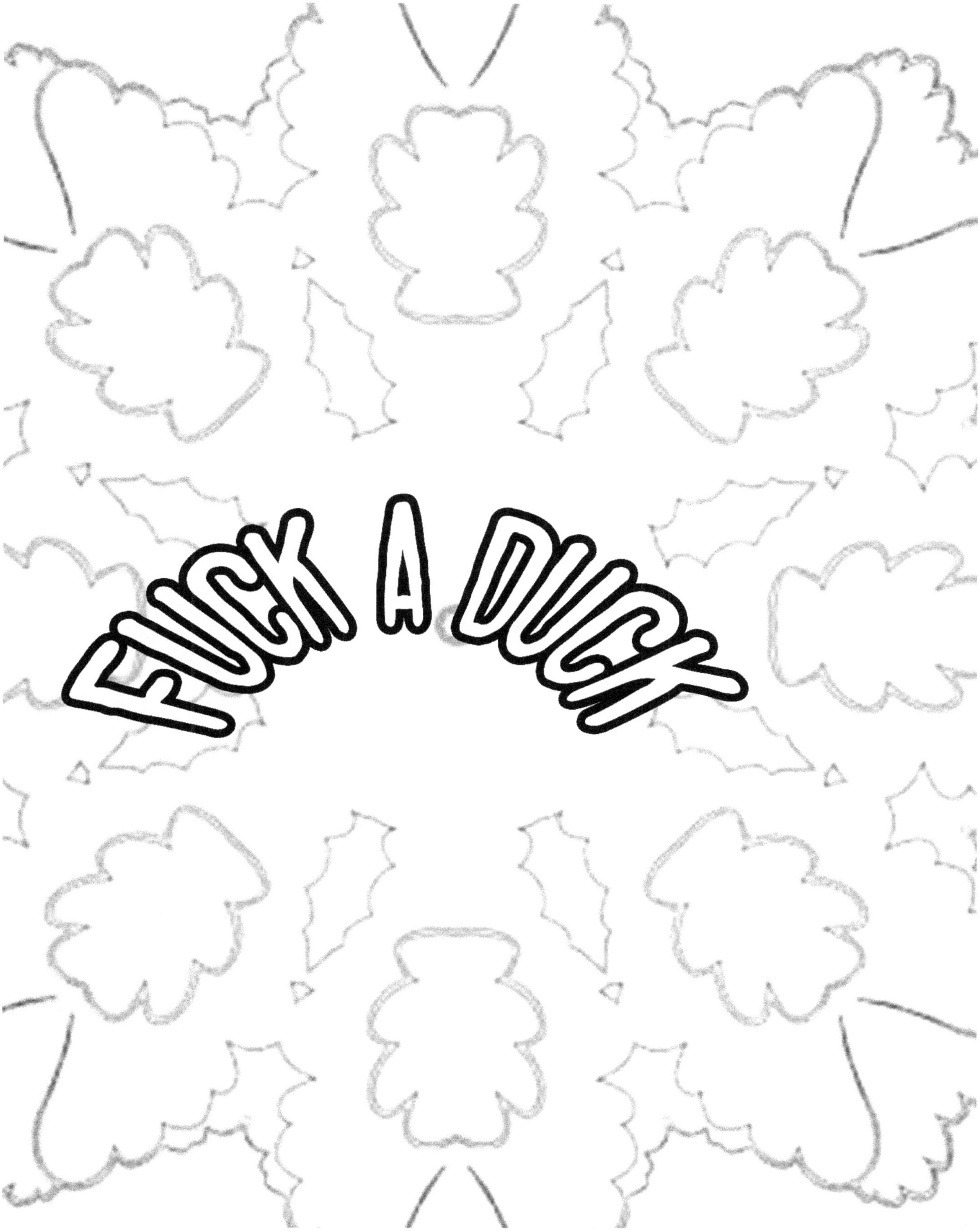
FUCK A DUCK

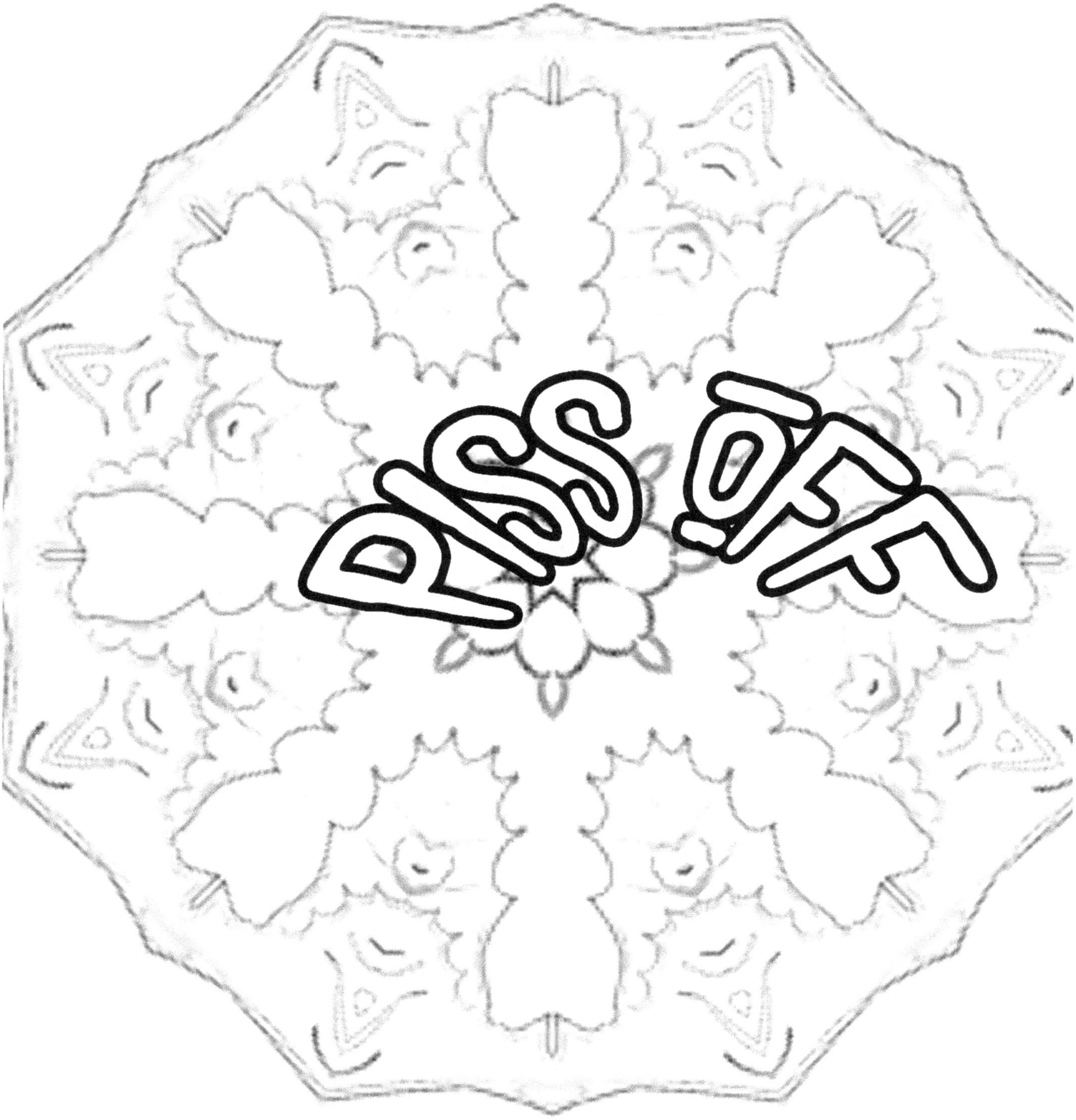
PISS OFF

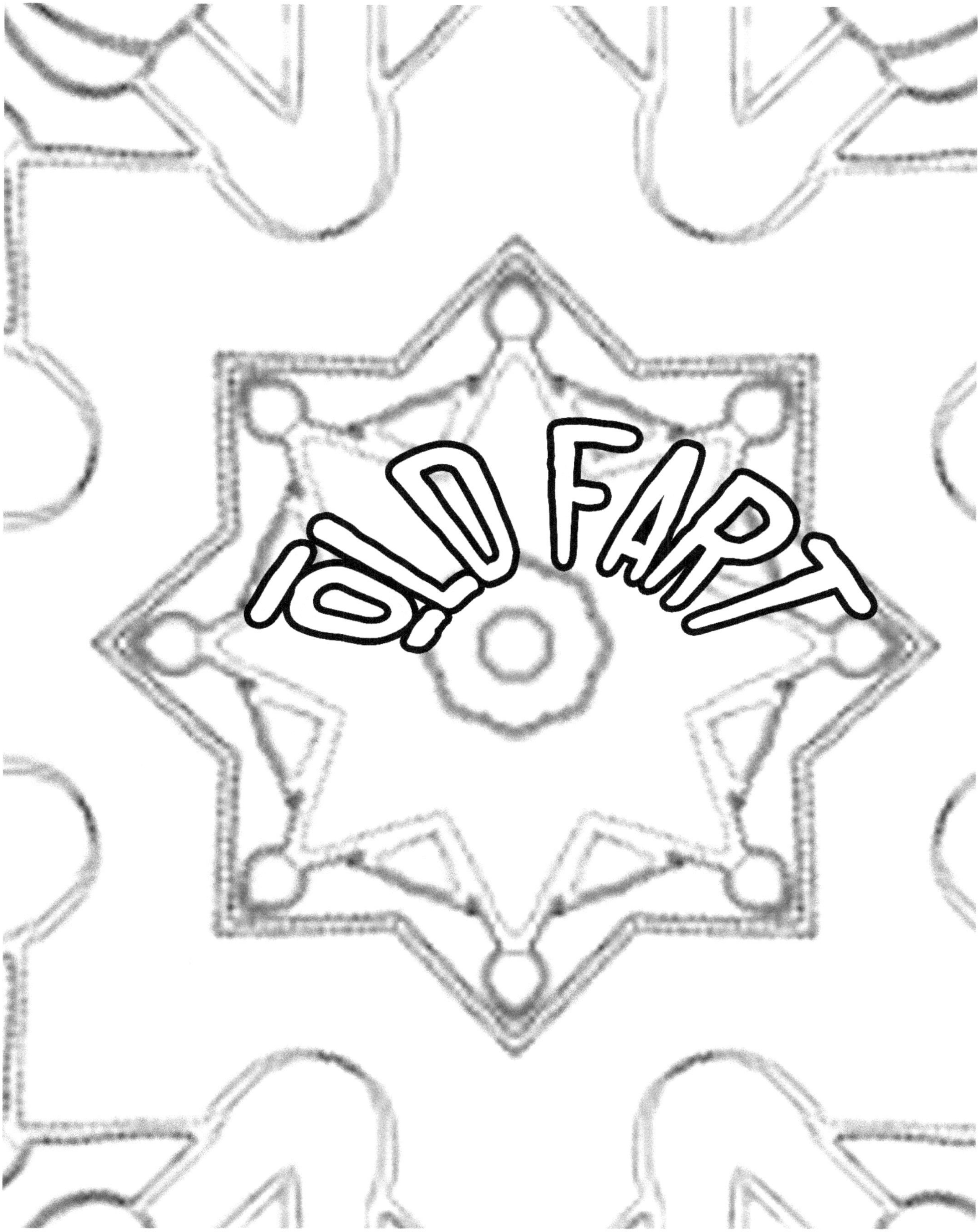
OLD FART

www.ingramcontent.com/pod-product-compliance
Lightning Source LLC
Chambersburg PA
CBHW081741170526
45167CB00009B/3901
9781542824620